8 Steps to a
SIZZLING MARRIAGE

by

DR. GILDA CARLE

Published in New York by
InterChange Communications Training, Inc.

ISBN-13: 978-1-881829-15-7

Library of Congress Control Number: 2015904241

Printed in the United States

For more information visit
www.DrGilda.com

ACKNOWLEDGMENTS

Thank you to all who have so generously contributed your true stories to help others who are reading this book. Without your giving, there would be less healthful living!
--Dr. Gilda

Gilda-Gram®
**For marital longevity, honor the
YOU and the ME,
but also the WE**

CONTENTS

INTRODUCTION

The Sizzlers vs. The Fizzlers

Marriage is a puzzle to many people. Although it's often repeated that the divorce rate is 50%, a survey reported in The New York Times says that the rate "has never exceeded about 41 percent." While it's heartening to know that the rate of divorce is not really as high as most people have believed, if you're among that dreaded 41% of couples with a marriage on the rocks, you're plenty miserable. Then again, if you're unhappy, yet choosing to remain married nonetheless, you're *doubly* miserable. Are you one of those people who need a marital turn-up, what are your feelings and fears, and how can you improve your troubled merger before it derails?

There are 2 kinds of couples in the world:

•*Those who make their marriage sizzle*

and

•*Those whose marriage fizzles.*

If you fall into the first category, you probably are not reading this book right now. But if you are in the second group, and you know your marriage needs a tune-up, this guide will quickly get you back on track.

Who are the Sizzlers?

Sizzlers are couples that give each other prime time. They recognize that even a healthy, solid marriage can derail if a husband and wife expend most of their time and attention on other people and things outside their personal bond. Of course, the kids must be tended to, and so must chores, work, relatives, and friends, but Sizzler Couples know when and how to put each other and their relationship above all else.

Who are the Fizzlers?

Fizzlers are couples who put other people and things before each other. As two people begin to disregard and ignore each other's needs, over time, each begins to feel angry and abandoned. This is when boredom with the marriage sets in. Some Fizzlers choose to stay (with their marriage) and stray (with an affair). Others choose to stay (with their marriage) and pay (emotionally, physically, and financially) as their unhappiness climbs.

But there is hope!

<u>Gilda-Gram®</u>
A couple that once had sizzle
can always rekindle it.

Dear Dr. Gilda,

My husband and I have been married for 12 years. It's a second marriage for him and a third for me. We are very close, and we love each other very much. But lately, all we do is sit at home like couch potatoes growing mold. At this point, we almost have nothing to say to each other. Even our lovemaking has become infrequent and dull. We need a drastic change!

Usually, he returns home from work before I do. Last night, as I walked in anxious to see him, AS USUAL, my husband was wasting away in front of the television, nibbling on candy, and totally unresponsive to me. I wondered why I had even come home! I was even more annoyed when he barely mumbled, "Hello, dear, how was your day?," obviously not even expecting a response. I immediately turned off his program. He hit the ceiling. What's wrong with what I did to try to regain the spark we once had?
Missing the Good Old Days

Dear Missing,

You're not only missing the "good old days," you're missing a beat in Relationship Etiquette! You are treating your husband like an old, well-worn shoe, ripe for kicking around. Turning off the program he's intently watching after he's just returned from a tough day at the office is not an expression of love and respect; it's a hostile act. Are you trying to quash your husband's source of comfort in his own castle?

If you think this kind of behavior will get him to lust for you, think again! Girl, the only way to re-ignite that fire you once enjoyed is to show your man you feel fire for him. Shutting off his TV has the opposite effect, more like dousing him with cold water. Ouch!!

The fact that you'd like to communicate as soon as you step into your home while your guy needs to relax first is one way our genders differ. Men and women see communication in very different ways: deep talk for a woman binds her to her man, while deep talk for a man causes him to feel stressed. This is where nature dealt partnerships a severe blow. Basically, the tendency is:

Gilda-Gram®
**Men feel invaded and
women feel evaded.**

So each person must understand and respect the gender differences we live with.

Missing, you need to try this new approach:

Gilda-Gram®
To get love, give love.

And I mean give love, not hostility. Here's a loving gesture you might try to get your guy to remember the passion you once shared. Next time, before you're about to come home, call him. Ask him how he would like to spend the evening with you. Plan an actual date night.

When you get home, if he's chilling in front of the tube when you walk in, respect that, and let him enjoy his peace for a while. In fact, even offer to get him a cold drink. Then be quiet and leave him totally alone. Unlike the female species able to multitask without taking a breath between chores, men need to unwind after work before they can even think about their mate's desire for marital bliss.

You've got to get him to want to want you— and you won't do it by kicking him in the TV tube! So if you'd like him to change the channel, you'll have to change your own channel first.

Gilda-Gram®
Show *com*passion for his needs, and he'll show *passion* for yours.

You once had the passion. Now that you know what you must do, grab it back with gusto!
Dr. Gilda

Missing's question is not unusual for people who have been married for a while. Sadly,

Gilda-Gram®
The primary complaint among marrieds is BOREDOM.

To eliminate boredom from your marriage, invest a brief 7 seconds, and learn the 7 anti-boredom principles below. Notice that each begins with a letter that, when combined, spells the word "Respect."

Gilda-Gram®
Without Respect, there can be no love.

Respect was what Missing was truly missing when she disrespectfully turned off the television her husband was watching. Respect is also one of the major components that guarantee a marriage's shelf life.

STEP #1

Use the 7-Second Boredom-Buster

R-E-S-P-E-C-T is your key to a sizzling marriage!

R EGARD your spouse as a *guest* in your home, instead of the traditional old shoe.

E XPECT the most from yourself, but accept your spouse *as is*, without criticism.

S HARE your embarrassing feelings, and find humor in them.

P ROTECT each other verbally and emotionally when you're with family and friends.

E XPERIENCE one untried adventure together each week.

C ONSIDER each moment you share as a *gift*, not just a usual day.

T ELL your spouse often why he makes you proud.

Busting up your boredom is your first step to returning the sizzle to your fizzle. The next step is to stop looking at what you consider to be the "greener" grass of your friends and neighbors, believing that their marriages are more solid than yours. If you dig deep enough, *you might be in for a big surprise!*

STEP #2

Discard the "Oh!-What-I'm-Missing" Factor

Most people begin their marriage with insatiable passion. But over time, they become very comfortable with each other as they settle in. They develop a new kind of familiarity . . . and, as the saying predicts, this familiarity breeds contempt.

Sex begins to take a back seat to other important things in a young married's life: a new house, a baby, in-laws, friends, relatives, and job pressures. *Does this sound familiar?* Eventually, in the mentality of "the-grass-is-always-greener," a misconception crops up that everyone else is having more fun and intimacy than they are, and they believe
they're missing out on something everyone else has.

This "Oh!-What-I'm-Missing" factor adds self-induced pressure to keep up a front of marital bliss to the outside world. *But all that glitters is not gold!*

Arlene was involved in a quickly fizzling marriage. Both she and her husband Fred had been divorced before so they wanted to avoid the pains of another split. So to continue the image, they worked hard to appear as a happy couple. They traveled to distant places, they bought new matching cars every two years, and they appeared as though they were living a life to be envied. But that was anything but the truth.

Insightful onlookers noticed a particularly outstanding clue as to what was really going on beneath this couple's roof. Arlene, an art aficionado who also loved to shop, had a unique passion for collecting pairs of exotic masks. Wherever the couple visited, she would buy another set to display on the wall of her, yes, "her" perfectly decorated home, because she had taken over everything in this house, totally discounting input from her husband.

Gilda-Gram®
Masks *mask* reality.

Arlene spared no expense on her purchases, and the beautifully displayed collectors' items boasted the couple's visits to every continent in the world.

But beneath the illusion, the couple felt huge animosity for each other, and when they were alone, their verbal put-downs never stopped. They slept in separate bedrooms, they ate at different times, and when they weren't traveling, they spoke to each other infrequently.

In public, Fred belittled Arlene often. Yet, she tried to dismiss the importance of his horrible remarks.

Secretly, she admitted she was not quite strong enough to leave. In fact, she irrationally feared that she wouldn't survive on her own, although she had a high-paying job, and enough money to survive well.

Throughout their hostile relationship, bullying Fred took to writing emails to his wife as his usual form of conversational complaint about the most insignificant things. For example,

Subject: Apples
Arlene,
Today I ate a second one of those apples you bought. These apples are big, soft and mushy, exactly the kind I don't like, and not even close to my continued request for small, hard, and tart ones. So again, unless you plan to devour them yourself, throw them out, along with the pork and chicken hot dogs you have in the refrigerator, which you know I don't eat. Obviously, you lack consideration for my preferences.
Fred

Arlene would typically write back to Fred in similarly angry tones. He'd respond to her, then she'd respond back, and on and on. The piles of nasty emails grew, and one wondered if that was all this couple had to do in their lives.

For years, Arlene continued to take the dance of anger in stride, camouflaging their furious dislike for each other beneath the masks. She chose to imagine that no one knew the truth, but family and friends often remarked that this "paradise" was not all it seemed. So whom were they fooling?

This couple's hostility might have continued forever, if not for one foreign stranger. On their last trip to Japan, after Fred made another of his usual demeaning comments to Arlene, their Japanese tour guide turned to him and asked why he continued to be so abusive to his wife! What? Suddenly, Arlene was taken aback! She was astounded that a total stranger, who did not speak English as her primary language, was able to see through the smoke and mirrors that for a long time, Arlene had been carefully crafting what to do next in this marriage. That one last remark seemed to do it! As soon as they returned home to the United States, she immediately sought an attorney and filed for divorce.

All the glitter you see is not necessarily the gold you think it is. Discard the "Oh!-What-I'm-Missing" Factor and realize you're probably missing nothing at all. Focus on all the positives you have going for you, and savor each one.

All couples experience good days and bad days, and in order to catch the sizzle before it turns to fizzle, a pair must consciously navigate the challenges of daily life. When you're married to someone, you don't just wake up in the morning, and say whatever comes to mind, disregarding your partner's feelings. Nor should you live a make-believe Hollywood fantasy with partners who matter little to you.

Real people need to make real choices to treat their mate respectfully and lovingly. That might become a tough order when the babies are crying, the car doesn't start, and you're petrified that your job will suddenly be downsized. But,

<u>Gilda-Gram®</u>
If you don't beat the blahs,
the blahs will beat you.

Always hold the reins of your romance so you can return it to the way it used to be before you slipped into the negative attitudes of cozy and cocky. Arlene and Fred had sizzle when their marriage began. So what happened that caused "hot" to become "not?" Step #3 will explain.

STEP #3

Know Why You Attracted
Who You Attracted

You are at a party and you see someone from across a crowded room. You feel instant attraction. You're convinced it's love at first sight. Well, *lust* at first sight does exist, but it's not the same as deep and lasting *love* that can only grow with time.

Gilda-Gram®
Love at first sight is merely
lust with potential.

Lust consists of brain chemicals that mix around in your head and produce "irrational highs." You find yourself walking into walls, becoming breathless when your new love calls, or getting butterflies in your stomach when you even hear his name.

As time goes on, you may notice that this person is your complementary opposite. But you like that. After all, if you're a morning person, for example, aren't you intrigued with how a night person functions? Unconsciously, you mistakenly believe that your two opposites are separate halves that are necessary to make you a great whole. Or, as the character in the Jerry Maguire movie erroneously announces, "You complete me."

Even with the smoke and mirrors of Hollywood, *no one can complete anyone else.* During the start of love, you may also sense that your partner has some traits, both good and bad, that you can identify in your own parents. Again unconsciously, the bad traits are usually more influential in your attraction because this gives you the opportunity to re-live and heal your old childhood wounds.

Also contributing to your craving lust to your partner is the gender issue: If you're a man, your new love sports good looks that you unconsciously think of as "good genes" for future children. If you're a woman, you unconsciously seek a partner with the ability to finance your offspring.

Gilda-Gram®
Mate-searching men seek *honey*.
Mate-searching women seek *money*.

And so it is. You lust after someone you don't yet know, but who reflects opposite traits to yours, which intrigue you, but which, since they're opposite, could also make you crazy as time goes on. Your new love also demonstrates qualities that unconsciously remind you of your most difficult parent so that you can re-script your childhood. While the familiar is enticing, the memories of that difficult parent can create stress once the relationship unfolds.

Meanwhile, your brain chemicals overpower you, and you're breathless, excited, unfocused, and unable to eat or sleep. For want of another description, you call the feeling "love." But it's merely lust with the potential of something more—if other elements line up.

You are in no position to rationally judge your future with this partner because you're temporarily "out of your [chemically-induced] mind." But you're unaware of how off-center you are. The familiarity of your new love's traits beckon you, and your desire to right the wrongs of your childhood are all too inviting. The only problem is that these motives are occurring unconsciously, without your awareness that they're even driving you.

But after you're settled into the relationship in a calmer way, the original forces begin to gnaw at you as you recall your childhood events, your inability to deal with them as a young person, and how you felt while they were occurring. More and more, your partner becomes the whipping post on whom you take out your past frustrations. Allegedly, he is a safe haven on whom you can dump your leftover emotions, because, after all, you unconsciously reason, he loves you, and you believe he'll remain with you no matter what abuse you heap on him.

What you don't count on is that he is experiencing his own childhood memories, the ones that also drew him to you.

He doesn't want to be your whipping post. How much abuse will anyone stand? As soon as a couple takes each other for granted, they could be headed for disaster, or, at least, an affair.

Therefore, the moment you sense that something is going awry, have the courage to converse about it. Issues don't evaporate on their own. And every person wants to feel he's got a cheerleader who will love him, no matter what!

STEP #4

<u>Understand Your Affair Potential</u>

Can lust last? Thankfully, it can't! If it did, we'd be constantly exhausted. Fortunately, romantic love only lasts from 18 months to 3 years. Then, something even better emerges in HEALTHY relationships. A more stable and calmer *friendship* takes over which is more rewarding and enduring than the walking-into-walls frantic pace you experienced earlier.

However, if your relationship is dysfunctional, and if you don't know any better, you misconstrue your new calm for boredom. Since the passion has slowed, you believe the love is gone. Worried about getting older and losing your sexual edge, you desperately search to renew the frantic passion you once enjoyed, but this time, *in the arms of someone new*.

This is the reason many affairs begin. It's the desire of a bored partner to renew his or her youth. You are now in a tizzy to recapture the feelings you once associated with the beginnings of marital bliss.

At first, a new lover fills you with those same initial feelings of early lust. And the excitement of sneaking around behind the back of convention adds to the illusion. But if you continue your sexual dance for another 18 months to 3 years with your new partner, you become overly comfy and the same boredom eventually sets in. Then, in an effort of re-claim that crazy-time passion, you're off again to search for yet another partner who can once again quench your lustful thirst.

If you're exhausted just reading about this constant quest for attention and stroking, imagine if you're the one involved in this charade. Its theme song is the Rolling Stones' tune, "I Can't Get No Satisfaction," played again and again and again.

True to human nature, everything new is exciting, even if it's only a new shirt. So imagine how exciting an all-encompassing new romance can be. But a continuous need for emotional caressing is impossible for anyone to supply. No one can *keep on* satisfying you in the passionate way you began each encounter. If that person did, you'd feel smothered, and you'd both be ready for a hospital!

Instead of driving yourself toward one new partner after another, all with the same predictable ho-hum results, understand that early lust, when followed by deep friendship, is the healthy relationship pattern a marriage needs in order to last. Of course, it can also work the other way around, beginning as deep friendship and blossoming into hot and passionate lust.

But open your eyes! Friendship does not signal death, as so many people erroneously believe. Just because you enjoy best-friend status the likes of which you've never known before, it does not mean your marriage is over, and you'll never again feel the heat of night! It's totally up to how much effort you and your partner are willing to invest in your union.

Gilda-Gram®
Marriage and passion
do NOT cancel out each other.

You may need to realign your thoughts. If you have (mis)believed that friendship has no place in an equation that involves heat, think again! For ANY bond to survive over time, friendship MUST be an ingredient.

Gilda-Gram®
After building friendship, you've already achieved
the hardest part in sustaining love!

Yes, constructing your friendship is the hard part. The love and heat will follow because of the solid respect you two people have for each other.

Just knowing this prepares you to plan a Sizzle Strategy. With this Strategy, you'll recognize the meaning behind a flickering spark. You'll know that this flicker alerts you to get your relationship back on track when it looks as though it's falling off the rails and entering a potentially "boring" phase.

And the best news is that the 4-Phase Sizzle Strategy only involves four steps to make your romance vibrant again. But you and your partner must be fully willing to commit to each.

STEP #5

Apply the 4-Phase Sizzle Strategy

Phase 1: Re-visit your flirtatious dating days.

Gilda-Gram®
Play together to stay together.

The Jerry Maguire myth of your partner "completing" you must be banished. In order to have a healthy relationship, each person must first be complete on his or her own. Each must know what he enjoys, and each must already have a *complete* life pursuing it.

Many couples come together because their last relationships ended in grief, and they're hurting, or lonely, or afraid to be alone. But just like taking o a new exercise regimen, people must be in top emotional shape before they take on a mate. No one should ever expect his or her partner to take up the slack he or she lacks. Only after you have fully learned how to enjoy playing when you're alone, will your own enthusiasm become an infectious ingredient in a partnership.
Phase 2: Share your deepest secrets.

Gilda-Gram®
Confide in your mate to build trust.

At first, a new couple is on their best behavior, and they are reluctant to share hurtful secrets they feel will mar their image. But once two people become accustomed to married life, they get to know each other in more meaningful ways than just their superficial attractions. Since one unconscious reason people come together is to fill the gaps left by their childhood wounds, understand that eventually the truth will emerge. Don't be surprised to discover that your partner is as emotionally barren as you are!

So what is needed is deep and honest communication between the two of you. Your mate had no idea that he was being called upon to put emotional tourniquets over your scarred past. Nor had you any idea at first that he was also still grieving his childhood wounds.

As painful as it seems to bring up buried secrets, they must be discussed if you want a lasting relationship. Both of you must be honest and vulnerable. Of course, that takes courage—and you won't display it if you don the kinds of masks that Arlene and Fred had been wearing. But such discussions also draw two people closer and builds trust between them. Trust is mandatory if you want to build a future.

Phase 3: Accept Your Spouse "As Is"

<u>Gilda-Gram®</u>
Leave the interior designing to interior designers.

Some Singles accept their mates while they're dating, yet as soon as there is a commitment, they want to re-do them, renovate their clothes, and even get them to think differently. What makes anyone think his/her pretty good partner should be molded into a better one? Well, you're hearing it here: leave your mate alone!! Like those garments on the clearance rack that are marked "As Is," accept your partner as perhaps a bit ragged or soiled, but someone you love nonetheless.

Once you stop trying to change him, you'll be able to spend your free time enhancing *yourself* and *your interaction with your partner*. Acceptance "As Is" is a major turn-on to any mate.

Phase 4: Deliver frequent and honest praise that makes your spouse feel good. When he feels good, YOU feel good!

Gilda-Gram®
Praise your mate honestly.

The *delicious* atmosphere that naturally builds after two people have been together for some time can also be accompanied by a feeling of being taken for granted. If this feeling is not acknowledged and kept in check, it can signal the beginning of a downward spiral.

Have you ever come home after getting a new haircut, or wearing a new shirt, or using a different kind of make-up, only to get no acknowledgment from the person you live with? It's occasionally happened to every married couple—and it's a sign to get more in sync with your partner.

Really *notice* the person you love. Offer honest flattery when he looks great or when she achieves something special. While you may have gotten into a comfortable living arrangement, just trigger the memory of how you *used to* react when love was new. Yum!!

When these 4 Phases are followed, a once-sizzling marriage could be re-heated in as much time as it takes to turn on the stove! Too bad the following couple did not know about these Steps before their marriage began to derail.

Hello, Dr. Gilda,

The last weeks have been an absolute nightmare for me. Three weeks ago, my wife of 5 years confessed that she was having an affair with her manager at work for 5 months. She developed feelings for him, and she said she thought she loved him. I mistakenly thought our marriage was wonderful. I guess I was wrong.

We went to a counseling session, which was not much help, so we discontinued it. My wife said the other guy made her feel special, and he spent a lot of money on her because he's rich. After I found out, I hardly slept or ate, I cried constantly, and I went through emotional hell.

Now my wife says that she wants to be with me, and that she is looking for another job so she can avoid seeing her lover again. She hasn't worked in two weeks (she works off commission), but she recently did go to work and bumped into him. She said they got into a heated argument.

The worst problem for me now are the images that flood my mind picturing her being physical with this guy. Those images are so present that I have been having trouble focusing at work, and I have also become distant toward my wife when we're at home.

I have always tried to be the best husband I can be. I laid tiles and a wood floor, I painted walls, spread topsoil, planted flowers, and everything I could do around the house. I'm even attending graduate school so I can get a promotion at work. But nothing was enough. Whenever I offered her love and affection, I was pushed away. She's just not affectionate—as least with me. I love my wife, but she really damaged me. We own a home together, we have three kids, and a divorce would not be simple.
Grieving Husband

Dear Grieving Husband,
Whether property and kids are involved or not, divorce is never simple—or easy on the nerves—for anyone! Why didn't counseling offer you some comfort and relief?
Dr. Gilda

Dear Dr. Gilda,
In our first and only session, we discussed why my wife's affair happened. My wife had many complaints about me. She said I never make decisions on my own, that I always base my actions on what she

wants, that I don't make enough money, I don't help writing the bills, and I'm very messy in the house.

Then she told me that her affair was just a thrill. This guy has money and he was showering her with gifts. She wasn't making high enough commissions, so he just handed her money to do with as she pleased, and she got hooked.
Grieving

Dear Grieving,
It sounds like your counseling session was not a bust at all. Think about it. It opened a necessary door to discussion, although it was certainly painful. Honest sharing should have been part of your marriage from the beginning. In that way, she could have shared her concerns, and together you could have considered options. Working on a relationship problem together can bring a couple closer since the two people are striving toward a common goal.

If you continue counseling, your wife will learn that there are no free handouts, and that everything has a price. She will learn that she can't blame her cheating on all the things you are not. I suspect you took her words to heart, and that's why you feel "damaged."

Now you both must prepare a new strategy. And you should have help doing that so you can prevent yourselves from remaining stuck with your angry images and thoughts. If the counselor you saw was not the right one for you, find someone who is.

Your wife was apparently bored and scared that

21

her life was not exciting. So she drummed up excitement on her own! Since she is blaming you for her own indiscretions, and you guys no longer have a counselor to guide her thinking otherwise, I advise YOU to get help on your own. You've got to pump up your self-confidence and discard the "damaged" feelings so both you and she can deem you an equal contributor to this union, rather than someone who is just there to please—or excite.

You shouldn't ever have to feel the need to defend who you are or what you earn to someone who loves you. If your wife wasn't doing well at her job, and she was unhappy with the money you are earning, an option would have been for her to take on a better-paying job, instead of taking on the boss. This is how a couple plans a strategy, and goal-setting for your future is one of the things your relationship lacks.

Your wife's affair can either be a wake-up call to work on the relationship, or a wake-up call to put the marriage to sleep. Whichever you choose will take great effort on both your parts.
Dr. Gilda

Gilda-Gram®
**Adultery doesn't always terminate a marriage.
65% of unfaithful mates remain together.**

Marriages used to suffer from a "7-year itch." The term was such a popular catchphrase that it became the title of a 1955 comedic movie starring Marilyn Monroe. The storyline depicts a faithful husband whose family goes away for the summer, while he becomes tempted by a beautiful neighbor. Thus, the seven year period in a couple's marriage traditionally signaled a time that was shaky, eventually threatening the shelf life of their relationship.

These days, in a world that seems to be more time-crunched than the 1950s, the number of years it takes for most marriages to derail has now crept down to only four! One researcher actually found that the 7-year downturn time still exists, but that it is now pre-empted first by a dip in the quality of a marriage during the fourth year.

These findings support those of the Census Bureau that determined the average marriage lasts only eight years. So we surmise that after the two marital dips, at both four and seven years, people finally decide to terminate the relationship during Year Eight. Then again, it was found that 43% of unhappy marriages break up at Year Fifteen.

So miserable people may hang in *miserably* for eight to fifteen years. How would you want to spend eight to fifteen years in a miserable marriage?

How can we reverse these statistics and the sadness of the couples crushed by marital derailment? Step #6 explains about the additional "person" in your marriage.

STEP #6

Honor the 3 "People" in Your Marriage

Gilda-Gram®
Examine your language!
Include YOU, ME, and WE.

When a couple marries, they believe that they only have each other to consider. Nothing is farther from the truth. There are three distinct "people" in every relationship. The two most obvious ones are the You and the Me. But once you embark on happy matrimony, there is yet another "person" to consider. It is a separate entity called the relationship, or the "We."

No longer, as you did when you were Single, or even dating, should you be speaking in terms of just You or Me. When a couple is focused on the We, they recognize that sometimes these two pronouns must take a back seat to the relationship itself.

Caring for all three "people" can be a real challenge, what with children, life stress, and the pressures of earning a living. What's required is a real balancing act, and honest and continued sharing to assess your progress. At all times, a task nearly impossible, each of the 3 "people" wants to feel acknowledged, supported, and loved.

Many marriages on the skids consist of only ONE self-involved person, with the other unhappily hiding in the shadows. For Grieving Husband, marriage meant happily pleasing his wife while he snuffed out his own needs. But his wife got bored living with a "Yes" man.

Rather than confront her feelings, however, she sought comfort elsewhere. She rationalized that her affair was due to her husband's shortcomings, rather than her unwillingness to confront her grievances. By the time the situation came to light in their one therapy session, her husband was left feeling "damaged."

If they truly want to start fresh, Grieving Husband and his wife will have to open the feelings they are resistant to discuss. As you can see, if honest feelings are not acknowledged and communicated, disaster will occur.

For sure, this is a balancing act: you don't want to confront every grievance you have, yet you don't want your feelings to just sit inside you and stew, making you sick or even fat. You want to be an independent person even within your marriage, yet you also want to show your mate you're very much in sync with him, and that you honor the "We." *Whew, lots to juggle!*

Both parties in a marriage must share their feelings, but they also must keep their individuality intact. An independent spouse is an asset to a marriage because she can bring adventure and new views to a routine that could possibly become boring. Yet, some spouses become so independent that they have almost a separate life. That's when a spouse begins to wonder what he's even doing in the marriage.

Dear Dr. Gilda

I'm so over love! My husband just left me because he claims I don't love him enough. Before I met him, I could not find a guy who could handle me having an opinion. I'm confident and independent, and I don't want to hide who I am anymore. I want to travel, learn French, and become an actress. I believe in myself. Why is that wrong?
Confused Wife

Dear Confused,

In order for a marriage to maintain excitement, two partners must maintain their individuality. Otherwise, both people will become bored or resentful when one partner consistently takes the lead. But how much isolation can any husband handle? You talk about wanting to travel, learn French, and become an actress.

The question is whether there is room left for a husband among your other goals. If a partner believes he will need to take a back seat to your dreams, he may feel unnecessary and disposable. Do you really believe your husband left on his own, or do you think you had a hand in "pushing" him out?

While you talk about your own goals, what are his? For a marriage to work, both people must strive for their dreams—but they must also consider how the

other fits into them, and how their dreams fit into their entire relationship. One-sided marriages don't make it past the lust stage.
Dr. Gilda

At the beginning, and usually for some time, many one-sided marriages are actually *supported* by the person in the shadows. Of course, that person desperately wants to be loving—and loved. For that reason, the more dominant partner believes that all is well.

However, eventually the Shadow Spouse builds resentment for the mate who isn't contributing to her happiness. She rightly tires of holding up the fort on her own. Because the couple may have remained in this dance pattern for some time, when the Shadow Spouse finally walks, her partner can't fathom what happened!

Dear Dr. Gilda,
I'm 32 years old and have recently broken up with my wife of two years. Honestly, I hadn't been the nicest partner to her. I was using drugs and alcohol and took a lot out on her instead of dealing with my own problems. I went to prison for 2 months and was released a month ago. The whole time, I was thinking about my wife and how much I love her. But she was thinking about how much she needed to get over me.

When I got out, I expected things to be the same between us. Now she doesn't want anything to do with me any more. I feel rejected and worthless. I need her more than anything. She was there for me before when times were tough, so why can't she be there for me now?

I am torturing myself and I am very depressed. I have never felt so bad. It feels like a part of my soul was torn away and I can't get it back. I wish I could show her I'm changed and that I will be the man she always wanted me to be. I regret everything I have done. Please help!
Smarter Now

Dear Smarter Now,
Some people need a kick in the head to grow up. You apparently are one of them. We all do stupid things, but look at how much you've learned! Perhaps you blew it with your ex forever. But that doesn't mean your life is over. Re-read your email to me. Notice that it's all about YOU and YOUR hurt feelings. I wonder how your ex felt when you weren't "the nicest partner to her."

The next growth step you must take is to get over your own misery, and understand another's. Whether you can get your ex to want you again is anyone's guess. Right now, think positively and show whomever you attract in the future that you are a stand-up guy.
Dr. Gilda

Dear Dr. Gilda,
Your email is right! I have been too concerned with my feelings and how it was always "me, me, me." I was so caught up in myself that I overlooked the way my wife felt. I wasn't there when she needed me most, and in turn, she's not there for me now. I have learned an extremely important lesson. A relationship is a two-way street.

You are right, I did need a kick in the head to make me realize what was going on. I recently attended an Anger Management class. I met a man there who was abusive to his wife. I saw a lot of myself in that man, and it was then that I promised myself to
treat others with respect and dignity. I appreciate your honesty in showing me that life is not always about me.
Smarter Now

Dear MUCH, MUCH, MUCH Smarter Now,
WOW! If every person who walks the face of the earth were as willing to grow as you, we'd have a much more peaceful world. God bless you! You'll probably make a great partner in the future, not only because of all you've been through, but especially because of all you've learned. Please let me know.
Dr. Gilda

Some folks learn from their mistakes like the emailer above. But others continue to make the same errors again and again and again. Roger, a college professor, was divorced for 10 years before he found Kate. After he asked Kate to marry him, he presented her with a 200-page, ironclad pre-nuptial agreement. The man had several million dollars from a family inheritance, as well as from his own stingy ways. And okay, he was rightfully looking to protect his assets, and he had a personality that customarily dotted every "i." *But 200 pages outlining when his wife would be permitted to burp during their marriage?*

However, because Kate had just left an abusive husband, and because she didn't take enough chill time to be alone, she misread Roger as a breath of fresh air, and especially as her "savior." *(The myth of Jerry Maguire lives on!)* The pair immediately fell into the early blush of lust that punctuates new romance.

While Kate hardly knew the guy, she nonetheless surmised that anyone would be better than her abusive, alcoholic, gambling, cheating ex.

Once the wedding ceremony was over, Kate began to see Roger's true self. He was cheap, cheap, cheap. He once even demanded she re-pay him for the $1.67 ice cream he bought for her teenage daughter. Kate also saw how Roger's cheapness extended into his inability to give of himself with her family, her friends, and her children. He was controlling and demanding, and moreover, he could only love *on condition* that he would get something in return for the little he gave. Everything in his life was weighted and weighed.

Gilda-Gram®
**Conditional love is a business agreement,
NOT a love relationship.**

Money is one of the biggest sources of discord among most couples. To put a lid on the fighting over finances, some marrieds choose to conceal their earning and spending from their mate. One client came to see me and revealed that she was hiding her huge salary from her husband so as not to threaten his own meager earnings. I told her that her marriage was fizzling. She did not want to hear that, and swore to me that I was wrong.

Six months later she was divorced. She finally conceded that it was too stressful to keep her marital lies alive in hopes of saving her husband's pride. She vowed that if she ever married again, their money status would be fully disclosed.

Soon Kate tired of Roger's cheapness. But she didn't want to admit defeat in having failed in another marriage. So she continued her misery beyond the Census Bureau's average eight-year stint. It was already ten long and painful years that the couple had remained together. The last straw came after Kate realized she was internalizing her grief. She suffered severe neck, shoulder, and back problems, no doubt brought on by the burden of *shouldering* her extra emotional cargo.

However, Kate's physical ailments got her to see the light. When she finally left, she wondered what took her so long to exit from such a self-involved, selfish, and angry man. *Sometimes a brick must hit us before we finally open our eyes!*

While I strongly advocate that two people honor the "We," a balance is nonetheless needed with the other two "people" in the relationship. If a pair devotes themselves *solely* to each other to the exclusion of the world, their relationship investment can become dangerous.

Dear Dr. Gilda,

When I grew up, my parents instilled strong moral principles in me. Although I didn't especially like the people who attended our church, I attended services every Sunday anyway. A young guy by the name of Ron started attending church on Sundays, too. In Ron's eyes, I stood out among all the girls he was meeting. I didn't go out of my way to be popular or to get people to like me. While others continued to engage in hurtful gossip, I just kept to myself.

Ron and I started dating for three years. The majority of my so-called "friends" at church tried to stop our relationship by introducing Ron to other young women, telling him that they could offer him more than I could. Ron wouldn't hear of it. We married three years later, and we've had a wonderful stretch of 17 years, including a very successful national business. We stick to ourselves, and because of my earlier experiences with so-called "friends," I have Ron as my husband and best buddy, and no one else.

Our two children are now in their teens, and they bring home plenty of pals. But as far as Ron and I are concerned, we have each other, and that's the way I prefer it to stay. Do you think this kind of isolation is healthy for a married couple?
Happily Married

Dear Happily Married,
Yours is a beautiful story about succeeding in love despite opposing forces. But you and Ron need to expand your social circle. It's wonderful that you have each other and can trust in other so deeply both personally and in business. However, while this

interdependence is a great aspect of what you both share, it can also be dangerous.

My popular book, "Don't Bet on the Prince!" notes that you can love "the prince," cherish "the prince," and make him a priority, but whatever you do, don't bet on him to give you breath! No spouse wants to consider horrible things happening, but sometimes a partner will die, get ill, or leave. So it is never advisable for you to be functioning as an island all by yourselves.

Please protect yourself and find even a few girlfriends you can trust. Since trust is such a difficult issue for you, you ought to begin by getting to know just one person at a time. That also means that you must eventually reveal your vulnerability to your friend after you feel fully at ease. Don't be in a hurry, because building deep friendship with the right people takes time!

Unlike a lot of folks who have trouble giving, your mission is to learn how to receive caring from outsiders. While you say that your kids already have many friends themselves, it's important for them to see how to expand their social circles. This is a life lesson. Begin it as soon as you can.
Dr. Gilda

Gilda-Gram®
**You can't love
if you won't receive.**

How can Happily Married expand her social life? You saw that the one-sided marriage is dysfunctional because it focuses on just one ME. You also saw that when a Shadow Partner focuses on that one ME, the YOU does not get emotionally fed and eventually will leave.

Yet, you also know now that it can be dysfunctional if a seemingly healthy two-sided marriage boasts a WE to the exclusion of everyone else. When the WE in your relationship is used as a buffer to "protect" you from others who may hurt you, while you may feel safe in the short run, you will also be missing out on a wealth of experiences, and people will be missing out on you.

So what is really needed? The answer is to support the three distinct "people" that comprise your marriage. Taking care of all these "people" can be a challenge, what with children, life stress, and the need to earn a living.

The question each couple must ask is, "How can we be sure that each of those three "people" feels acknowledged and loved?" The answer is to continue to observe each of these different "people," and focus on the one that hasn't received much attention lately. Since you'll need to spend much time observing, the benefit is that while you're on your toes, you'll never be bored!

Acknowledging the three "people" in her life with her husband, Elizabeth was very smart in how she coped with her stressed-out man. She said, "My husband's work wipes me out, and him, and us." She clearly recognized the issue as affecting all three "people." At first, she tried lecturing him about finding a new job. Then she tried telling him how deeply his stress was affecting her. Neither of these approaches worked.

So she prepared a candlelight dinner to erase his thoughts of work and focus on their romance. During their meal, she said absolutely nothing about his job. They laughed and talked extensively about everything except that. She was showing him a part of "We" that the couple had long forgotten.

His job stress and *her* grievances meant little compared to the glorious interaction they had that night. In the end, their "We" won out; the husband began looking for another job only one day later, and without prompting from his wife.

Gilda-Gram®
Demonstrating sizzle
may prompt your partner to change.

As you can see from what happened with Elizabeth, talk is cheap, but *showing* hits deep. Showing compassion demonstrates what your model relationship looks like. And because you are part of the demonstration, it proves that you're emotionally present to him.

Gilda-Gram®
Emotional presence is a strong aphrodisiac.

When you show your mate that you're emotionally *there*, he feels a unity of the two of you against the cold, cruel world. *That's true security!* But to be emotionally present, you must be willing to discard the veils, yes, those gauzy protectors you've been hiding behind each time you wanted to feel safe.

STEP #7

<u>Show Your Vulnerability</u>

Are you willing to reveal your true self?
Complete *"Am I In Touch with My Feelings and Fears?"*
below, one of my most popular Self-Assessments. It's
short, quick, and very revealing.

<u>Am I In Touch with My Feelings and Fears?</u>

Fill in the blanks to this ONE question:

The most difficult feeling for me to show my spouse is
_____ because I'm frightened that _____.

<u>Self-Discovery</u>

Did your responses surprise you? Why?

<u>Carolyn wrote</u>: "The most difficult feeling for me to
show my husband is fear because I may become
vulnerable and be left to his mercy. I don't show my
spouse my vulnerability because I'm frightened it might
be misconstrued as a sign of weakness, and I'm not a
weakling!"

<u>Robert wrote</u>: "The most difficult feeling for me to show

my spouse is being afraid because I'm frightened she will laugh at me."

Leila wrote: "The most difficult feelings for me to show my spouse are when I'm upset and about to cry, and also my most intimate feelings, and finally, my insecurities. I don't show him that I have dreams and goals because I'm afraid he may speak negatively of them."

Paula wrote: "The most difficult feelings for me to show my spouse are fear and trust because I fear I might be betrayed."

Bill wrote: "The most difficult feeling for me to show my spouse is love because I'm afraid that she might get the upper hand and toy with my emotions."

Ralph wrote: "The most difficult feeling for me to show my spouse is that I need her because she will think I'm needy and have no pride, which will hurt and humiliate me."

These responses all came from married people. Marriage is supposed to be a partnership where you feel comfortable enough to share your true feelings without feeling that you'll be ridiculed. If you can't let down your proverbial hair with your spouse, then with whom can you?

A group of respondents I was working with sat in a circle and read their replies on their Self-Assessments. Suddenly, one woman burst into tears when she said she had to admit how concealing she was in her marriage. A man said it was very sad that he feared being betrayed by his own spouse. Another man remarked that this Self-Assessment showed him that his marriage was in trouble. He said that he now knew why he was constantly depressed.

After completing this Self Assessment, respondents are often shocked that they have been in marriages for some time, yet still feel the need to protect their true emotions. Walking on eggshells is no way to live.

Gilda-Gram®
Healthy marriage frees you to be yourself—
warts and all!

When you feel free, you don't have to second-guess your mate, wonder whether you can trust her, or feel the need to control her every move. She, in turn, feels that freedom with you, too. Trustworthy partners know that they're there for each other no matter what. Unfortunately, the following emailer doesn't have that peace of mind—especially at a time when he needs it most!

Dear Dr Gilda,

I am a 25-year-old male in the U.S. Army stationed in Iraq. I met this beautiful Mexican girl three months before I was leaving for South Korea. We were instantly inseparable. I reported in to South Korea, and about three months later, I called her. When she answered the phone, she started to cry. I asked what was wrong, and she said that she had been waiting for me. We talked and talked, and began having a long distance relationship. I went on leave to visit her. Her parents loved me, and wanted us to get married. I had never thought about marriage before. We talked about it, and we did tie the knot.

It was time for me to go back to Korea for another year. I asked my new wife to move to Korea with me and she agreed. Once she got there, she hated it. They wouldn't let her finish school or work. We fought a lot, I went into the field for thirty days, she felt abandoned, and then she tried to commit suicide. She then returned to the U.S.

We worked out our differences and we were good and strong. We have been married now for 2 years. Dr Gilda, I love her with all my heart. I went on leave and I spent tons of money on myself, which put us into pretty bad finances. Suddenly, she told me it is over. I was crushed.

She said that for these years she took my verbal abuse, and now that I think of it, she was right. I used to call her dumb and stupid, but a lot of times I was playing. I tried to win her back. I told her I would change and I would stop spending money and I have. I also watched what I said to her. I called every other day because I was worried about our marriage. I bought her an $800 necklace. She took it back, and she told me that she doesn't want me to call her anymore, but she swears that I am the love of her life.

Dr. Gilda, I tried to take my life when she told me to leave her alone. My wife hasn't emailed me or called. Even though we have never lived together as husband and wife, I want my marriage back. I realize I have done wrong with verbal abuse, money spending, and even walking out of the room when my wife would cry. I guess I'm just young and immature. What do I do now?
Miserable

Dear Miserable,
It is so sad that you must go through these wartime life and death experiences, and I deeply feel for you. During crises, people don't think rationally or logically. To add to your situation abroad, you are right: you and your wife are both young and immature. Grownups don't threaten to commit suicide when they don't get enough attention from their partner. But it also shows how dependent you have become on having this woman as your wife.

The war, your separation, the quick courtship followed by a quicker marriage, the interruption of your personal goals, and your financial mess would bring any marriage to its knees. You've never lived together as a married couple, yet you want to play house like grownups. Most marriages begin on a much more positive note.

I strongly recommend that you take a breather from each other until you are together in the same geographic locale. Then see if you are feeling anything more than lust. Currently, you find yourself not only in the midst of a real war, but engaged in a war at home, too. That's too much stress for anyone to endure.

After you're back, go on dates with your wife, and s-l-o-w-l-y assess whether this marriage is even worth saving. Let your heart guide you, and then have the courage to do what it tells you--whatever that may be. Reach out to me if you need some help!
Dr. Gilda

Dear, dear readers, after reading this, aren't you glad you thought your biggest marital woe was merely boredom?!! There are thousands of military marriages in our country and partners are feeling grave stress. In fact, I've been so moved by the numbers of military people who contact me because they desperately need this help, I've created a non-profit organization (Country Cures at www.CountryCures.org) to treat the relationships of our returning veterans. And we do it with Country Music, America's favorite music genre. So you might want to explore our services. At the very least, find a relationship expert near you who you trust to help you deal with this debacle.

As you can see from all I've said, marriage requires constant attention and nurturing. So imagine the additional factors of war and all that brings, including the fear of not knowing whether you and your spouse and children will ever be together again. Imagine the need to be uprooted often, and the uncertainty about all the basics civilians like us take for granted.

This outreach especially moves me because our service people and their families protect us with their own lives, and I feel that the least we can do is give back to them and their families when they return home. If you know military personnel or veterans who need relationship building, please send them to Country Cures. We've already helped thousands.

The same sort of marital stressors that exist in people who serve during war time occur when you or your partner has a life-threatening disease, or your home has been ravaged by natural disasters like fires, hurricanes, landslides, or floods, or when you face the constant threat of terrorism.

There are numerous other horrendous occurrences people face. Sometimes they marry quickly, like Miserable above, in an unconscious effort to set up some security around their unstable life. Other times, they cheat without thinking, or divorce quickly, in a conscious effort to flee the scene of their misery.

In whichever way they choose to deal with their difficulties, people try to cope with their circumstances in the best way they know how. They thirst for salvation and peace somewhere, and in so doing, they often make decisions that are not well thought out. If they allow their unconscious to drive them, when they finally do achieve calm, they find themselves having to pick up the pieces of the mess they made after they've signed on the bottom line. Is putting temporary bandages on a deep wound worth the price it costs?

Are you considering marrying someone right now? Many people don't take the needed time to think what their future with their chosen partner would look like in only a few years. If you're one of those people, please, please talk to a relationship expert before you take the plunge.

STEP #8

<u>Know Your Date Before You Mate</u>

By this time, after learning all you have, read this last email below. How would you rate the odds of this relationship making it in marriage?

Dear Dr. Gilda,

I have been dating George for almost 2 years now. He has been divorced for about a year, but he's been separated from his ex wife for 2 years, and he has custody of his 4-year-old son. During our relationship, we broke up for about 4 months because I found him cheating on me.

But a few months later, he asked me to forgive him because he did not want to lose me. He said he knew I was worth a lot. After we talked, we got back together. Since then, he changed and everything was great.

About a month ago, I went into his computer and found an email from one of his friends describing some X-rated movies they watched. When I confronted him, he said he watched for a few minutes and then left the room. We have been talking about moving in together and taking our relationship into marriage. However, I feel insecure about it now. He reassured me that he loves me and wants to be with me.

To make matters worse, out of nowhere, I received a letter from his ex-wife detailing all the times he cheated on his exes and on her. She also sent printouts of porn sites he uses to look for women.

Dr. Gilda, I'm really confused and I'm not sure of our relationship anymore or whether I should move in. When I confronted him about it, his response was that not all women are the same, so he just likes to look to compare. Please help!
Confused

Dear Confused,
This is more a question of how much you know about this man than about whether you should move in together and marry him. You are very smart to be scared about your next move. Girlfriend, this is your LIFE! Making wise decisions now will prevent you from suffering great heartache later.

Your guy never had time on his own without a woman. Just because he has custody of his four-year-old son does not make him a mature male—or even a good potential husband. Being separated from his wife for 2 years is not the same as being divorced from her.

<u>Gilda-Gram®</u>
**A *separated* couple is busy defining their
past together and their future apart.
If you're a Single, stay away.**

*So although a couple in the midst of separation
may be living apart, by necessity, they are still
emotionally joined. You entered the scene before your
guy had time to breathe on his own. That means that
you became part of the drama of his splitting up.*

*Relationships that begin this way usually have an
expiration date of "soon." A person divorcing is
wounded, and you would have to play the role of nurse.
That would not make for two independent people joining
together, which is a necessity for a healthy union.*

*Now that he's on his own with his son, based on
his ex's letter to you (and how did she get involved in
this mix, anyway??), he's resumed what appear to be
similar behaviors to those that brought down his
marriage. You're scared because your gut is flashing a
"CAUTION!" sign—and rightly so. I always advise
people to trust their gut.*

*You say you love this dude, but I question
whether you know this dude! What makes you think he's
changed? What incentive is there now for him to start
fresh? You just uncovered more things about him than
you care to know. Why not wait to formalize your
relationship until you feel emotionally safe? Do you
want to continue to be snooping around his email and*

other private things, wondering what else he's been concealing? Look, this guy could be perfectly wonderful but he likes to "look" at porno. Most men do. But if this is something that upsets you, he should not become your man.

I say chill a while, and continue dating, but don't live together. After you trust him more, you'll be better equipped to decide your next move.
Dr. Gilda

Gilda-Gram®
If you're afraid of marriage, or have some doubt, love YOURSELF—and do without.

CONCLUSION

If You Don't Control the Sizzle, Your Marriage Will Fizzle

You are in the driver's seat. You can make your relationship a partnership that combines hot passion with deep friendship. Contrary to all the chiding you may hear from marital failures, "matrimony" never has to mean "boredom," and "monogamy" never has to mean "monotony."

Make your marriage shine! Surround yourself with couples that enjoy a glorious life together, and pick up their cues. Notice the respect they demonstrate. Those are the new friendships you should nurture, and those are the people whose traits you should mirror. Believe you deserve a sizzling marriage and you will build one. It's totally in your hands. And I'm always here to help guide your success!

***

Benefit from
Dr. Gilda's personal Advice & Coaching
www.DrGilda.com

MORE BOOKS BY DR. GILDA

Dr. Gilda's Self-Worth Series
-- I'm Worth Loving! Here's Why.
-- Ask for What You Want—AND GET IT!
-- How to Be a Worry-Free Woman

Dr. Gilda's Relationship Series
--8 Steps to a Sizzling Marriage
--8 Tips to Understand the Opposite Sex
--10 Questions Single Women Should Never Ask
      & 10 They Should
--10 Signs of a Cheater-to-Be

Dr. Gilda's Fidelity Series
--Why Your Cheater Keeps Cheating—And You're
Still There!
--How to Cope with the Cheater You Love—and WIN
--99 Prescriptions for Fidelity: *Your Rx for Trust*

ALSO
--Don't Bet on the Prince! *How to Have the Man You Want by Betting on Yourself*
--Don't Lie on Your Back for a Guy Who Doesn't
Have Yours

***

Dr. Gilda Carle (Ph.D.) is an internationally known media personality and relationship expert. She has authored 15 books, including "Don't Bet on the Prince!" (a test question on "Jeopardy!"), "Teen Talk with Dr. Gilda," "He's Not All That!," "How to WIN

When Your Mate Cheats" (winner of The London Book Festival literary award), "99 Prescriptions for Fidelity," and more. She also wrote the weekly "30-Second Therapist" column for the Today Show, and the "Ask Dr. Gilda" advice columnist for Match.com.

On TV, Dr. Gilda was the regular therapist for the Sally Jessy Raphael show, the "Love Doc" for MTV Online, and the TV host of "The Dr. Gilda Show" pilot for Twentieth Century Fox. In addition, she was the therapist in HBO's Emmy Award winner, "Telling Nicholas," featured on Oprah, where she guided a family to tell their 7-year-old that his mom died in the World Trade Center bombing.

In academia and the corporate sector, she has been a management consultant, Professor Emerita, motivational speaker, and product spokesperson.

As President of Country Cures, Inc., a non-profit 501(c)(3) educational charity organization, she is the "Country Music Doctor." As such, the organization uniquely uses country music to provide education and training for transitioning veterans and their families. If you, or someone you know, can benefit from this help, please see www.CountryCures.org.

Reach Dr. Gilda at
www.DrGilda.com
or
www.CountryCures.org

www.ingramcontent.com/pod-product-compliance
Lightning Source LLC
Chambersburg PA
CBHW071639040426
42452CB00009B/1697

*9 7 8 1 8 8 1 8 2 9 1 5 7 *